50 Maps

OF THE WORLD

ACTIVITY BOOK

WIDE EYED EDITIONS

WELCOME TO OUR

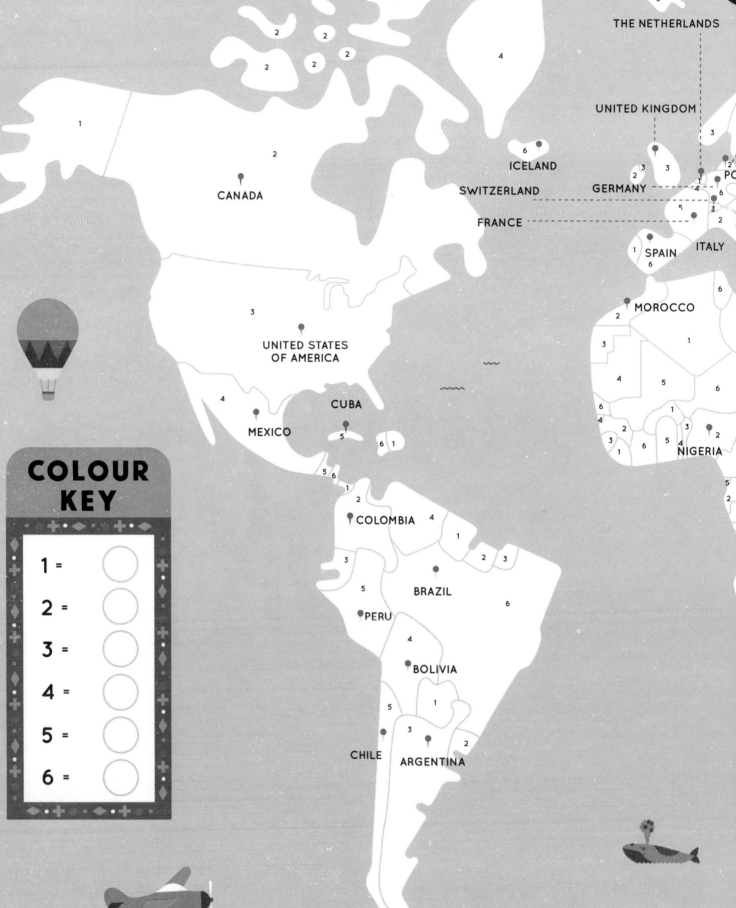

THE NETHERLANDS

UNITED KINGDOM

ICELAND

SWITZERLAND

GERMANY

FRANCE

PO

SPAIN

ITALY

MOROCCO

NIGERIA

CANADA

UNITED STATES
OF AMERICA

CUBA

MEXICO

COLOMBIA

BRAZIL

PERU

BOLIVIA

CHILE

ARGENTINA

COLOUR KEY

1 = ⬤

2 = ⬤

3 = ⬤

4 = ⬤

5 = ⬤

6 = ⬤

AMAZING WORLD

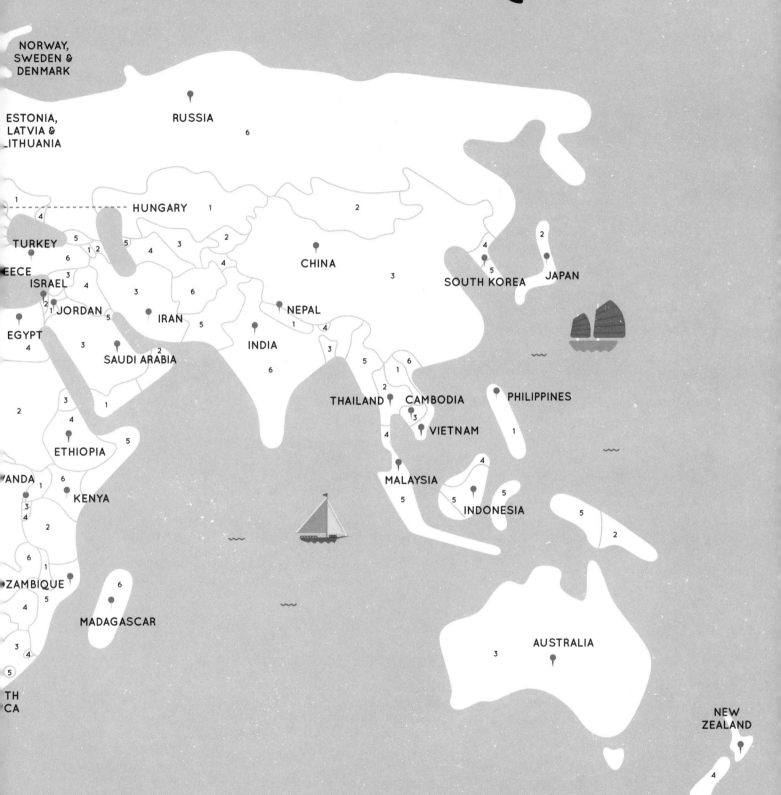

NORWAY,
SWEDEN &
DENMARK

RUSSIA
6

ESTONIA,
LATVIA &
LITHUANIA

1
4   HUNGARY   1   2

TURKEY   5   1 2   5   3   2
6   4
EECE   3   4   CHINA   3   2
ISRAEL   4   3   6   4   JAPAN
2   5   NEPAL   SOUTH KOREA   5
1 JORDAN   IRAN   5   1
EGYPT   4   INDIA   4
4   3   3
SAUDI ARABIA   6   5   6
2   1
3   2   1
2   4   THAILAND   CAMBODIA   PHILIPPINES
5   3   VIETNAM   1
ETHIOPIA   4
ANDA   6   4
1   MALAYSIA   5
3   KENYA   5   5   INDONESIA   5
4   2
6   2
1
ZAMBIQUE   6
4   5   MADAGASCAR
3   4   AUSTRALIA
5   3
TH
CA
NEW
ZEALAND
4

Our incredible planet is made up of nearly 200 countries which fit together like the biggest
jigsaw puzzle you've ever seen. Each country has its own fascinating history, unique climate, incredible
languages, colorful flag, and so much more. Travel to France and tuck into a delicious croissant, journey
to China to spot giant pandas, and marvel at the Mayan pyramids of Mexico! Every corner of the world
is different, which is what makes this planet we call home so wonderful. Are you ready for an adventure
like no other around our amazing globe? Pack your suitcase, get your passport ready, and let's go!

**Choose six different colors and fill in the color key on the left. Then color the map using
the numbers as a guide. You'll find that no two countries of the same color are touching—
and maybe learn a few new countries along the way!**

FLOWER POWER

Did you know that many countries around the world have their very own national flower or plant? These floral emblems are usually used as a symbol for each different country and are often linked to an area's history or culture that dates back hundreds or sometimes even thousands of years. Some national flowers are picked by their country's government, while others are chosen by the public in huge flower elections.

Use the most vibrant colors you can find to color in this selection of national flowers from across the world. Which one is your favorite?

Royal jasmine— Saudi Arabia

Shamrock— Northern Ireland and Ireland

Mountain avens— Iceland

Tribulus omanense— United Arab Emirates

If you could pick a flower to represent your country, what would it be?
Draw a picture of your national flower below—it can be real or imaginary!
Don't forget to give your flower a name too.

FAMOUS FOOD

One of the best parts about traveling to countries you've never visited before is trying out delicious and surprising foods. Some dishes are so loved by the people of a country that they have become a part of the national identity. Many are well-known and enjoyed around the world, too. A stew of beef, vegetables, and spices called goulash is the national dish in Hungary while Ireland is famous for its scrumptious potatoes!

Can you match the different foods below to the correct country?
Follow the squiggly lines to find out which food belongs to each country.

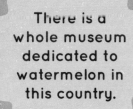
There is a whole museum dedicated to watermelon in this country.

WATERMELON

CANADA

These crispy scallion pancakes can be topped with seafood—delicious!

PAJEON

KOREA

This famous cheese is named after the town it comes from.

CAMEMBERT

CHINA

Creamy cheese curds, rich gravy, and fries make this a Quebecois classic!

POUTINE

FRANCE

DESIGN YOUR OWN MENU

If you could design your very own world menu, what would be on it? Draw pictures of the yummy things you would include in the space below. If you need inspiration, take a look at the picture bank of foods below and invent some delicious dishes of your own.

STARTER

ENTRÉE

DESSERT

PICTURE BANK

ANIMAL MAZE

A trip around the world means you're sure to see creatures big and small that you might not have come across at home. From slinking tigers in India, growling Tasmanian devils in Australia, and water-splashing elephants in Thailand, to soaring eagles in the USA, scuttling crabs in Cuba, and so much more, your adventure around the world spotting mighty and mini creatures will be anything but boring!

Can you find your way through the maze on the opposite page? Watch out for dead ends and misleading signs!

WHICH OF THESE ANIMALS DO YOU SPOT ON THE WAY!

FLAMINGO	SEA TURTLE	JELLYFISH
SHEEP	GIANT PANDA	SPOONBILL
BULL	RHINO	TIGER
DEER	STINGRAY	HYENA
MACAQUE MONKEY	KOMODO DRAGON	HUMPBACK WHALE
PEACOCK	CROCODILE	CRAB

START

This way
to the end

Go this
way

Follow this
path

FINISH

WORLD WORD SEARCH

It's time to put your country knowledge to the test! Can you find all of the country names in the world search on the opposite page? There are 20 to uncover, and they might be forward, backward, up, down, or diagonal. If you get stuck, use the word bank to help you. Don't forget to check your answers at the back of the book!

WORD BANK

FRANCE	MOZAMBIQUE	JORDAN	RUSSIA
MEXICO	KOREA	MADAGASCAR	ETHIOPIA
CAMBODIA	GREECE	IRELAND	JAPAN
INDIA	AUSTRALIA	COLOMBIA	SPAIN
GERMANY	CANADA	HUNGARY	VIETNAM

```
M N R E T H I O P I A F M A
A A U I N D I A A C O R A A
D P S Y N A M R E G R A O M
A A S R D N A L E R I N A O
G J I A I Y N M E X I C O Z
A D A N A C U O R F C E H A
S R A M N A D R O J A I U M
C N A I B M O L O C M G N B
A A I L A R T S U A B R G I
R A L A E R O K A C O E A Q
N M F T P D H O Q O D E R U
N S N Q E S A M X A I C Y E
V I E T N A M A T I A E N G
P I A I A G S J R N A F S O
```

JUMBLED UP BIRD NAMES

Official or unofficial, many countries around the world have their very own national bird. These national birds ruffle their feathers as they sit on the tallest branches, spread their wings wide and soar high across the sky, and dive through the many lakes and rivers that are scattered across our amazing planet. Sometimes images of these feathered friends appear on flags, money, and stamps.

The names of 15 national birds are all jumbled up on the opposite page. Can you unscramble each one to reveal the name of the bird? Use the word bank below if you get stuck. Check your answers at the back of the book.

WORD BANK

DANPHE	HOOPOE	EMU
BLUE CRANE	MUTE SWAN	TURUL
CUBAN TROGON	GODWIT	GIANT IBIS
BALD EAGLE	GYRFALCON	NIGHTINGALE
GALLIC ROOSTER	ROBIN	SHOEBILL

MY BEAUTIFUL BIRD

Do you have a favorite bird? What would you choose to be the national bird if you had your own country? Use the space below to draw your fluttery friend. It can be real or made up. Don't forget to give your bird a name too!

AGLCLI RORTEOS
FRANCE

NIBOR
UK

DALB ELGEA
USA

DIGOTW
THE NETHERLANDS

RTULU
HUNGARY

CFGRALONY
ICELAND

PADHNE
NEPAL

OPOHOE
ISRAEL

ETNGNIIAHGL
IRAN

GTANI BISI
CAMBODIA

ULEB NRECA
SOUTH AFRICA

TUEM WNAS
DENMARK

EHSIBLLO
RWANDA

ABCNU OGONRT
CUBA

UME
AUSTRALIA

TRUE OR FALSE NATURAL WONDERS

It's time to put your natural wonders of the world trivia to the test with these true-or-false questions! For each fact, circle whether you think it is true or false. Check your answers at the back of the book.

1. AURORA BOREALIS, SCANDINAVIA

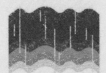

Aurora Borealis is the jet-black night sky in certain parts of Scandinavia, where not even a twinkling star can be seen.

TRUE OR FALSE

2. SOPPONG CAVES, THAILAND

Some of these 200 limestone caves, near the small town of Soppong, contain wooden coffins over 1,700 years old...

TRUE OR FALSE

3. MOUNT ETNA, ITALY

Mount Etna is an extinct volcano, meaning it hasn't erupted in around 10,000 years—and probably won't again.

TRUE OR FALSE

4. RED AND ROSE VALLEYS, TURKEY

These valleys get their name from the pinkish-red rocks, which turn a rosy color as the sun sets.

TRUE OR FALSE

5. GIANT'S CAUSEWAY, NORTHERN IRELAND

A giant named Finn McCool built the Causeway as a bridge to Scotland, so he could fight the giant Benandonner.

TRUE OR FALSE

6. MOUNT FUJI, JAPAN

Mount Fuji is also called Fuji-san, Fujiyama, and Fuji no Yama.

TRUE OR FALSE

7. MOUNT OLYMPUS, GREECE

Ancient Greek mythology says that Mount Olympus was the home to the 12 Olympian gods.

TRUE OR FALSE

8. HOLE IN THE WALL, SOUTH AFRICA

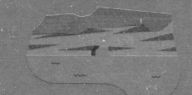

This rock formation is too small for an adult to swim through.

TRUE OR FALSE

9. THE BLUE LAGOON, ICELAND

This seawater spa is bright pink thanks to the algae that live there.

TRUE OR FALSE

10. MOUNT BROMO, INDONESIA

A volcano is active if it is erupting now or has erupted in the last 10,000 years.

TRUE OR FALSE

11. WHITE CLIFFS OF DOVER, UK

These chalky cliffs are roughly the same height as 20 male giraffes stacked on top of one another.

TRUE OR FALSE

12. NIAGARA FALLS, CANADA AND USA

Niagara Falls is actually made up of three different waterfalls.

TRUE OR FALSE

13. MONT BLANC, FRANCE

Mont Blanc is the smallest mountain in the Alps. It takes just six hours to climb it.

TRUE OR FALSE

14. LIVING ROOT BRIDGES OF CHERRAPUNJI, INDIA

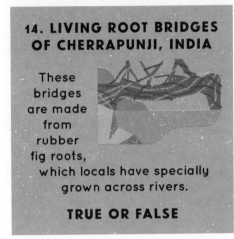

These bridges are made from rubber fig roots, which locals have specially grown across rivers.

TRUE OR FALSE

15. CHEONJEYEON WATERFALLS, SOUTH KOREA

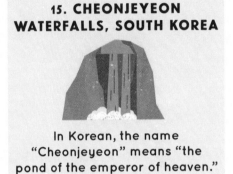

In Korean, the name "Cheonjeyeon" means "the pond of the emperor of heaven."

TRUE OR FALSE

16. VENTA RAPID, LATVIA

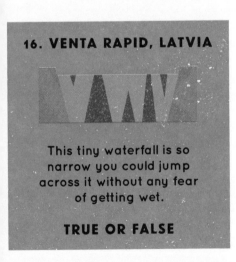

This tiny waterfall is so narrow you could jump across it without any fear of getting wet.

TRUE OR FALSE

17. STONE FOREST YUNNAN, CHINA

This "forest" is actually a formation of giant, 270 million-year-old limestone stalagmites.

TRUE OR FALSE

18. LAKE BAIKAL, RUSSIA

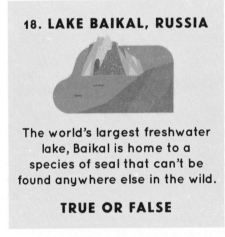

The world's largest freshwater lake, Baikal is home to a species of seal that can't be found anywhere else in the wild.

TRUE OR FALSE

19. THE MARBLE MOUNTAINS, VIETNAM

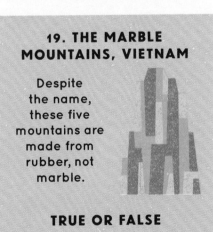

Despite the name, these five mountains are made from rubber, not marble.

TRUE OR FALSE

20. GRAND CANYON, USA

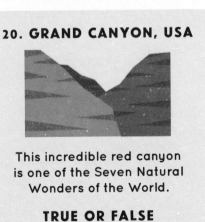

This incredible red canyon is one of the Seven Natural Wonders of the World.

TRUE OR FALSE

21. ULURU, AUSTRALIA

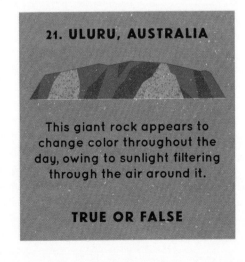

This giant rock appears to change color throughout the day, owing to sunlight filtering through the air around it.

TRUE OR FALSE

SPOT THE DIFFERENCE

Our amazing world is home to some truly fantastic people. These people of note have made it into the history books because of their incredible deeds, acts of bravery, brilliant brains, speedy records, creative flairs, and so much more.

Can you spot the differences between each row of pictures?
There is one difference per pair. You can find the answers at the back of the book.

MAHATMA GANDHI

AMELIA EARHART

NELSON MANDELA

CARLOS VALDERRAMA

CHARLES DARWIN

TAIHŌ KŌKI

VINCENT VAN GOGH

CLEOPATRA

TIRUNESH DIBABA

ALBERT EINSTEIN

SACAGAWEA

GRETA THUNBERG

WHO'S YOUR HERO?

My hero is _____ from _____.

They are my hero because _____

_____

Gandhi led India to independence from British rule.

Earhart was the first woman to fly solo across the Atlantic.

Mandela was South Africa's first black president.

Valderrama played football for Colombia for 13 years.

Darwin's theory of evolution changed science forever.

Kōki was considered the greatest sumo wrestler of all time.

Van Gogh created over 2,000 strikingly beautiful artworks.

Cleopatra ruled Egypt before its conquest by the Romans in 30 BC.

Dibaba has three Olympic golds in long-distance running.

Einstein developed many important scientific theories.

Sacagawea guided Lewis and Clark as they crossed the USA.

Thunberg began the global "School Strike for Climate" in 2018.

FLAG FINDER

Every single country around the world has its very own flag. The colors, pictures, and designs of each flag link to the religion, culture, or history of the country it represents. Some countries have a simple design on their flags like Ireland and Italy, which have three block colors, while other countries have much more elaborate designs like the United States, which has 50 stars to represent the 50 states of America.

Read the clues and try to work out which flag belongs to which country: Cuba, Peru, India, Rwanda, and Greece.

There is some red on Peru's flag.

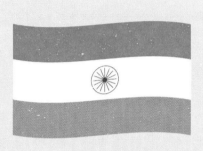

One of the flags with blue and white stripes is Cuba's.

Rwanda's flag features a star.

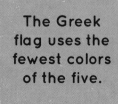

The Greek flag uses the fewest colors of the five.

India's flag has three stripes, and a picture in the middle.

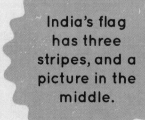

CREATE YOUR OWN FLAG

Imagine you had your very own country—what would you want your flag to look like? Would it be simple and just have a few blocks of color on it like the German flag? Would it be more detailed and have a wonderful picture on it like the Spanish flag? Or maybe it would have a pattern of stars on it just like the flag of the USA. Use the space below to create your very own flag. Take a look at the flags scattered around this page for some inspiration before you get started.

Write your country's
name here.

FIND THE HIDDEN MESSAGE

Adventures big and small await you on your tour around the world. From snorkeling in the crystal-clear waters of Brazil, to kayaking around Tierra del Fuego in Argentina, cliff diving in sunny Mexico, and taking a trip around a wildlife safari in Kenya, there is so much to do in every corner of our amazing planet.

Can you reveal the hidden activities below and opposite? Cross out every third letter to find out what adventures await you on your journey from country to country. Use the word bank on the opposite page if you get stuck. The first one has been done for you. Check your answers at the back of the book.

> You can dance a *sevillana* at the Feria de Seville in Spain.

1. DA~~X~~NC~~Y~~IN~~O~~G   D A N C I N G

2. SNFORUKEPLICNGQ   _ _ _ _ _ _ _ _ _ _

3. HIGKIANGU   _ _ _ _ _ _

4. ROTCKS CLVIMSBIANGW   _ _ _ _ _ _ _ _ _ _ _

5. SNBOWDBOPARSDIANGM   _ _ _ _ _ _ _ _ _ _ _ _

6. SUCNBBATFHIONGW   _ _ _ _ _ _ _ _ _ _

7. KASYAWKINNGM   _ _ _ _ _ _ _ _

> In Okinawa, Japan, you can snorkel with manta rays.

8. CYRCLHINSG   _ _ _ _ _ _ _

9. SCAUBOA DTIVUINLG   _ _ _ _ _ _ _ _ _ _ _

10. SUBRFOINVG   _ _ _ _ _ _ _

11. SWLIMCMIFNGA

___ ___ ___ ___ ___ ___ ___ ___

12. SAFILZINCG

___ ___ ___ ___ ___ ___ ___

13. STEARCGAFZISNGP

___ ___ ___ ___ ___ ___ ___ ___ ___

14. ICFE SIKAVTILNGB

___ ___ ___ ___ ___ ___ ___ ___ ___ ___

15. SKFIIGNGS

___ ___ ___ ___ ___ ___

You can white-water raft down Dunajec River Gorge, Poland.

WORD BANK

ICE SKATING	STARGAZING	SUNBATHING
HIKING	SNORKELING	SCUBA DIVING
CYCLING	KAYAKING	SAILING
SNOWBOARDING	ROCK CLIMBING	SKIING
SWIMMING	DANCING	SURFING

WHERE IN THE WORLD?

Every country in the world has its own unique history, languages, animals, landscapes, foods, sights, and sounds. All these things and more come together to create a culture—and a whole world of exciting experiences waiting to be had. Are you ready to test your knowledge of the world around you?

Can you work out the name of each country below? Read the clues and look at the pictures to help you.

This country is in Europe. It is the home of the croissant and the Eiffel Tower. To say "hello" here, you might say "bonjour."

This country is home to lots of unique animals, including the kangaroo, koala, and emu.

Thousands of years ago, this country was ruled by pharaohs. Today you can still see the monuments they built, like the Great Pyramids.

This country shares a border with the USA. Its food is loved all over the world—maybe you've tried tacos, burritos, chili, or nachos?

Explore the Amazon rainforest or dance to the sounds of Carnival in Rio de Janeiro in this South American country.

This country's flag is white with a red circle in the middle. Its capital is Tokyo. One of its most famous landmarks is Mount Fuji.

Stonehenge, Arthur's Seat, and Buckingham Palace await you in this country, often known by just two letters.

NUMBER PUZZLE

Our world is full of numbers! There are around 8 billion people living across the globe; our Solar System has eight planets circling around it; around 70% of the earth is covered in water; and the great wall of China is over 13,000 miles long!

**Each picture on the opposite page stands for a different number from one to eight.
Use your math skills to solve the sums below and write each number next to its picture.
Two have been done for you.**

 = 2

 = 3

WHAT COMES NEXT?

You're about to jet off on your whirlwind tour around the globe. What will you pack in your suitcase to take with you? You'll need an eagle eye for detail to help get you organized before you head off on your trip. Can you work out what comes next in the pattern below? Take a look at each sequence and see if you can figure out what comes next.

Use the space provided to draw or write what you think should come next. One has been done for you. Don't forget to check your answers at the back of the book!

From Ushuaia, Argentina, you can catch a cruise all the way to Antarctica.

Hong Kong's Victoria Peak tramway is so steep you'll feel like you're about to fall backward!

The Trans-Siberian railway runs through 85 cities and eight time zones.

In the Philippines, you can kayak the Puerta Princesa River from forest to sea... underground!

WISH YOU WERE HERE

No trip around the world is complete without sending postcards to your friends and family. Whether you've seen an amazing animal, explored an ancient ruin, or eaten the most delicious meal, there's always something to write home about!

Imagine you're traveling the world on an amazing adventure and you want to send a postcard home. Design your postcard in the top box, then write your message in the bottom box.

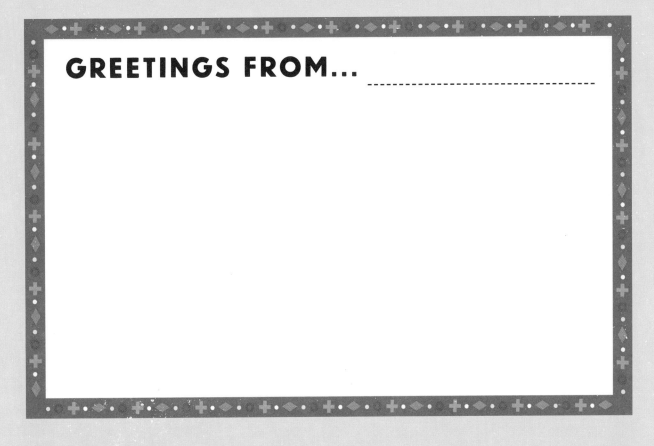

GREETINGS FROM... _____

ODD ONE OUT

Some places and buildings are so iconic that they have become symbols of their country, just like a national bird or flower. You wouldn't expect to find Buckingham Palace in Brazil, or the Great Wall of China in Ireland... would you?

Have a look at the rows of pictures below. In each one, circle the landmark that's from a different country to all the others. If you get stuck, use the hints to help you.

USA

HINT
The odd one out is a cathedral in Barcelona with many spires.

   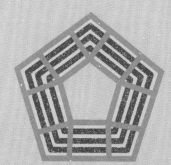

ITALY

HINT
The odd one out, the Sky Tower, shoots straight up into the sky.

 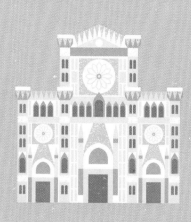  

UK

HINT
The odd one out welcomes visitors to Brazil's Rio de Janeiro.

JAPAN

HINT
The odd one out has four stories and high windows.

EGYPT

HINT
The odd one out is by far the most modern of the four!

FRANCE

HINT
The odd one out was designed to resemble the sail of a boat.

CHINA

HINT
The odd one out is known for its distinctive "pod" where visitors can look out over Toronto.

SPLiSH, SPLaSH SEARCH aND FiND

With over 70% of our amazing planet covered in water it's not surprising that our seas, oceans, rivers, and lakes are teeming full of watery wildlife.

Take a look at the watery scene below and see if you can spot an exact match of each picture in the box. There are eight to find. Circle each one, then check the back of the book for the answers.

PICTURE BANK

answers

Famous Food
Watermelon—China, Pajeon—Korea, Camembert—France, Poutine—Canada

Animal Maze

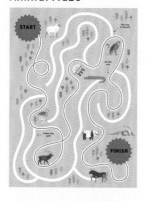

World Word Search

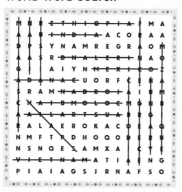

Jumbled Up Bird Names
Gallic rooster, robin, bald eagle, godwit, turul, gyrfalcon, danphe, hoopoe, nightingale, giant ibis, blue crane, mute swan, shoebill, cuban trogon, emu

True or False Natural Wonders
1. False! Aurora Borealis is a colorful light display caused by the North Pole's magnetic field.
2. True! The caves with coffins are known as "spirit caves."
3. False! Etna is one of the world's most active volcanoes.
4. True! The valley is in the famous Cappadoccia region.
5. False! The Causeway was formed by prehistoric lava.
6. True! Fuji is famous for its perfect mountain shape.
7. True! The Ancient Greeks told many stories of the Olympian gods and goddesses.
8. False! In fact, a boat could sail through the hole.
9. False! The Blue Lagoon is...blue, and good for your skin.
10. True! Mount Bromo erupted as recently as 2019.
11. True! The cliffs are on the southeast coast of England.
12. True! The three are American Falls, Bridal Veil Falls, and Horseshoe Falls.
13. False! Mont Blanc is the Alps' tallest mountain and can take three days to climb.
14. True! The bridges take 15-30 years to complete.
15. True! This three-tier waterfall is thought to have healing powers.
16. False! Venta Rapid is the widest waterfall in Europe.
17. True! Wind and running water shaped the rock into an eerie maze of tall, sharp pillars.
18. True! It's called the Baikal seal.
19. False! The Marble Mountains are indeed made of marble.
20. True! Everyone on Earth could fit into the Grand Canyon with plenty of room to spare.
21. True! Uluru features in many Indigenous Australian legends.

Spot the Difference

Flag Finder

Find the Hidden Message
Snorkeling, hiking, rock climbing, snowboarding, sunbathing, kayaking, cycling, scuba diving, surfing, swimming, sailing, stargazing, ice skating, skiing

Where in the World?
France, Australia, Egypt, Mexico, Brazil, Japan, UK

Number Puzzle

What Comes Next?

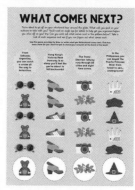

Odd One Out

Splish, Splash Search and Find

50 Maps of the World Activity Book copyright © Quarto Publishing plc 2021
Text copyright © Quarto Publishing plc 2021
Illustrations copyright © Sol Linero 2020
Based on the book 50 Maps of the World by Ben Handicott and Kalya Ryan

First published in 2021 by Wide Eyed Editions,
an imprint of the Quarto Group.
100 Cummings Center, Suite 265D, Beverly, MA 01915, USA.
T +1 978-282-9590 F +1 078-283-2742 www.quarto.com

ISBN 978-0-7112-6299-7

Designed by Sasha Moxon • Edited by Claire Grace • Published by Georgia Amson-Bradshaw

Printed in Illinois, USA. vR112023

10 9 8 7 6 5 4 3 2 1